God of th

'Modern Spirituality' series

Circles of Love
(Daily Readings with Henri J. M. Nouwen)

Creative Prayer
(Daily Readings with Metropolitan Anthony of Sourozh)

Day Trips to Eternity
(Daily Readings with Lionel Blue)

Gateway to God
(Daily Readings with Michael Ramsey)

The Joy of Being
(Daily Readings with John Main)

The Narrow Path
(Daily Readings with Dietrich Bonhoeffer)

The Shining Wilderness
(Daily Readings with Thomas Merton)

Treasures of the Heart
(Daily Readings with Jean Vanier)

The Universal Christ
(Daily Readings with Bede Griffiths)

The Watchful Heart
(Daily Readings with Ruth Burrows)

God of the Impossible

DAILY READINGS WITH CARLO CARRETTO

Edited by
Robin Baird-Smith
with an Introduction by
Mary Craig

DARTON · LONGMAN + TODD

First published in 1988 by
Darton, Longman and Todd Ltd
1 Spencer Court
140–142 Wandsworth High Street
London SW18 4JJ

Reprinted 1991 and 1996

British Library Cataloguing in Publication Data

Carretto, Carlo, *1910–*
God of the impossible.
1. Christian life – Daily readings
I. Title II. Baird-Smith, Robin III. Series
242′.2

ISBN 0–232–51752–5

Phototypeset by Intype, London

Printed and bound in Great Britain by
Page Bros, Norwich

Contents

Introduction

Carlo Carretto was, he says, converted to Christianity at the age of eighteen. His parents and parish priest might have been surprised to hear that, since to all intents and purposes, Carlo was a model Catholic boy. His devout mother saw to it, for example, that no criticism of the clergy ever passed his lips. Accordingly, he became, in his own words, 'an insufferable little bigot'. He recalls with painful clarity an incident which occurred in his village when he was eight years old, and which illustrates only too well the intolerance which at that time passed for normal among Catholics:

> One day a man came, going from house to house selling books . . . I didn't understand what was going on, but I heard the word 'Bible' spoken for the first time. A strange sort of agitation spread through the village, infecting the women first, and then everyone else, even the children. Suddenly a woman screamed, and from an open window came cries of: 'Barbet, barbet (the derisory way in which we Piedmontese referred to Waldensian Protestants), be off with you, we want none of your religion here.'
>
> The man walked along the street, his face pale, carrying his books in a large heavy satchel. A woman flung after him a book she had bought from him earlier, and without turning round, he bent to pick it up. Whereupon a boy hurled a stone which hit him in the back. The man accelerated his pace, followed by a crowd of

boys, each of them with a stone in his hand. One of those boys was me.*

Later that evening, at Mass, the parish priest congratulated the youngsters on defending the Church's honour. In those days, few would have been found to deplore such manifest wrongheadedness.

Though shuddering at that particular memory, Carretto recalls his childhood as a placid and unruffled time, and his parents as true Christians who passed on to him important fundamental values about life. But while he obeyed the rules of the static Christianity that surrounded him, his heart remained untouched.

Carretto was born in 1910, in Alessandria in Piedmont. His parents, from farming-stock in the Langhe hills, had found work in the town after freak June storms had devastated the hilltop farms. As a young child, Carlo heard the story of his parents setting out by night to walk sixty kilometres to the plain – and starting work on a new farm next morning. It was his first intimation that, with God's help, the bleakest catastrophe may be transformed into a light to steer by.

As an adolescent, Carretto had to struggle with doubts about religion. But faith took him unawares one day in Lent, when he was eighteen. While making his confession to an old missionary with eyes 'full of simple goodness', he felt a sudden, profound inner change: 'I was aware, in

* All the quotations in this Introduction are from *Carlo Carretto* by Teresio Bosco, *Collana Campione* no. 23, Editrice Elle Di Ci, 1983.

the silence of my soul, that I had caught a glimpse of God.' This new awareness was something qualitatively different from anything he had felt before, and he recognized it as a divine call:

> I have always noted that moments like that do not depend on ourselves. It is God making us take notice of him . . . It has nothing to do with intellectual understanding, it is something that floods one's whole being. I felt as though I were being clothed with the life, the light and the love of God. And in that moment of heightened awareness I became a Christian.

That was the first of three important watersheds in Carretto's life. 'God calls us at every moment of our lives,' he said later, 'but there are certain times in our lives when that call becomes more insistent and urgent.'

Carlo Carretto was a normal, healthy young man who, by the time he was twenty-three, had begun to think seriously about marriage. Until one day, during a chance encounter with a doctor acquaintance, the idea of a total commitment to the Church – as layman, not priest – was born.

He has no very clear memory of what happened next, but it seemed to him that for the second time God was making demands on him:

> Praying in a deserted church, where I had gone to escape the tumult of my thoughts, I heard the same voice that I had heard while confessing to the old missionary. 'You will not marry,' it told me. 'You will offer your entire life to me. I alone shall be your enduring love.'

More extravagantly, he claims that 'God burst in on me with his Spirit . . . He stormed in like someone madly in love and asked me to love him back with a total madness of my own.'

Then followed a period of strenuous, almost frenetic, activity: 'years filled with work, with passionate conviction, and with grandiose dreams. Even the mistakes – and they were many – were due to the violence of what burned inside me, a passion that was not as yet purified of self-interest.' Between 1936 and 1952, Carretto launched himself into work for Catholic Action, the militant organization established by Pope Pius XI, initially to counter the left-wing revolutionary ideas sweeping through Europe after the First World War; and later also to meet the challenge of rampant right-wing Fascism. Catholic Action aimed to present the Catholic Church's own social teaching (manifested in the encyclicals *Rerum Novarum* and *Quadragesimo Anno*) as a viable and attractive alternative to both extremes.

Catholic Action was immensely successful in Italy. And it made the name of Carlo Carretto, who in the course of time emerged as a natural leader on a high road to success. In 1948 he became leader of its important Youth section, at the precise moment when the Christian Democratic Party had won a massive electoral victory over the Communist Popular Front. The influence of the Church had never been greater, and within that Church few wielded a power greater than Carretto's. He represented a new and potent spirit of Catholic triumphalism, symbolized by the figure of Christ the King. He was 'somebody'. As he would say later, 'Jesus's words about humility and service . . . were lost on me. They always seemed to be meant for others, rather than for me.'

Carretto was so busy travelling, addressing workers' gatherings all over the country, that he had no time to stop and contemplate. Recognized as one of the most powerful men in Italy, he was nevertheless aware of a huge inner void which was gradually destroying his effectiveness. By the early 1950s, Carretto had lost all confidence in himself – and in the movement he represented. It sometimes seemed to him that he was as good as dead.

He was forty-four when the third and most serious call came: to the contemplative life. He heard the same voice as before, saying, 'Come with me into the desert. I do not want your activity any more. I want your prayer and your love.' And Carretto, though he did not at all understand, said, 'Yes, Lord.'

Though politics was the immediate cause of Carretto's leaving Catholic Action in 1954 – he objected to the way in which the Christian Democratic Party was trying to manipulate the organization for its own purposes – the determining factor was the spiritual one. 'I suddenly realized', he said, 'that both Italy and the Italian workers could manage perfectly well without me. The Church had more than enough militants. But what I needed was to probe the frontiers of the spirit. Of course I could have stayed with Catholic Action. But the power it offered was in danger of threatening our faith . . . History teaches us that when the Church is powerful, it is in danger of losing its soul. In the New Testament, there is not one word about power: Jesus speaks only of service . . . We were forgetting that we were first and foremost God's servants.'

Having come to understand, therefore, that 'the roots of true action lay in contemplation', Carretto laid down his power, said goodbye to his friends – and went off to join the Little Brothers of Charles de Foucauld in the Sahara. It was, he admitted, 'a step I took in faith rather than in reason'. Some found the gesture prophetic, others thought he was mad.

Years later, when a young man asked Carretto to define the contemplative life, he replied: 'To arrive at contemplation, you must pass beyond the frontiers of reason . . . Faith is born in darkness; and knowledge of God is truly a gift from God out of the darkness.' When we surrender ourselves to contemplation, he said, we are like 'a clean slate, on which God can trace the lineaments of Christ'.

What Carretto was turning his back on was the trap of easy living, of a soft and comfortable lifestyle: in his eyes, the curse of our times. A comfortable life exposes us to spiritual death, he insists: Western civilization is dying of its self-indulgence and excess. 'All the great religions were born between the desert and the steppe, where there is neither wealth nor destitution,' he tells us. 'We must do away with the extremes of poverty and wealth. In the middle is the true poverty of Jesus, the poverty that has just enough for its needs, but no more.'

Carretto found, in the desert, not the emptiness he had expected, but pure gain. As a gesture of renunciation, he was required as a novice to burn the large notebook containing the addresses of all his friends. 'It was the hardest thing I was ever asked to do,' he recalls. 'I can still see the charred remains being carried off by the Saharan wind . . . But the burning of a book does not imply the destruction of friendship. At no other time in my life did I love and pray for my friends as I did in the solitude of the desert.'

There, in the desert, he learned to pray – and to subdue his own will, growing in the understanding that 'it is not we but God who is the architect of our lives'. Like other well-intentioned Westerners who go to the Third World, imagining they have something valuable to give the dispossessed, he had to learn that it is not enough to put something into the begging-bowl; the really important thing is to stand in the line of beggars oneself, sharing and identifying with their sufferings. This, he insists, creates the only true solidarity with the poor.

Though Carretto must have believed that he would end his days in the Sahara, his superiors thought differently. After ten years he was ordered back to Italy. 'The desert is only for a time,' he concluded, not without sadness. 'We must return from it to the world of men.'

At Spello, on the slopes of Mount Subasio, Carretto established a prayer-centre where young men could come to pray 'in silence, and alone with God', dividing their time between prayer and physical work. He expected perhaps ten young men to join him in the contemplative life. He got a hundred; and over 1000 more applied to come. Eventually he was able to accommodate 200.

Carretto's famous *Letters from the Desert*, which expounded the attractions of contemplation, had instantly become a worldwide best-seller. Yet the question was often asked: Is the desert still important for the Christian? Is not the real work of today in the urban jungles? Though, over the next ten years, he wrote many books of reflection, he left the question unresolved until the autumn of 1978 after he had been to Hong Kong, that shrine to extreme wealth and the power of international commerce. There he found 'thousands of young workers wanting to talk about the meaning of life, about the Beatitudes, poverty and prayer'. They could not go to the desert; how then were they to find God in the city? For such as these, he wrote *The Desert in the City*, reducing his advice to two simple propositions:

> Wherever you are, at home, in the garden, in an attic, make a little oasis of peace for yourselves, where you can find God in silence and prayer. Regard everything in which you engage – work, meetings, walking, shopping, personal relationships, reading newspapers – as an activity through which God is speaking to us. You will find God in the concrete situations of daily life more effectively than by thinking pious thoughts.

What counts, he insists, is 'the continued, living, passionate communication with God'.

Carlo Carretto is still at Spello. In a way, he is more powerful than ever before, because of the thousands who read his books and try to follow his desert way. But his is now the power of the humble man. He does not regret his Catholic Action activist period – after all, it was 'the river in which I learned to swim'. But, where once he aspired to be 'first, for the honour of Christ the King', he now seeks to be 'last of all, for love of Christ'. As far as the Church authorities are concerned, he is something of a maverick. It is no secret that he would like the Church to change, to be more attuned to 'the signs of the times':

> The great, official, solemn Church, replete with ceremony, visible power and weight of numbers no longer impresses . . . People today know the anguish of loneliness . . . They are thirsty for love, friendship, personal relationship . . . More than anything else, they want a Church that nourishes them with God's Word, works with them by taking them physically by the hand . . . a Church that smells of beginnings.

He looks for priests who are 'not too busy to care', and provides his own definition of the ideal Church: 'a community of brothers known to one another by name, travelling with me along the road of faith and love'.

The Church may continue to preach of moral codes and sin, but to Carretto the only real sin is 'not believing, not hoping, not loving'. In a variation of St Augustine's 'Love God and do as you will', he counsels, 'Do not worry about what you ought to do. Worry about loving.'

Once we have joined the ranks of the poor, he assures us, we will become either an advocate of violent revolution or a St Francis. But he is no advocate of the former, for revolutionary violence ignores the needs of those who are poor here and now, for the sake of a hypothetical future. The message of Carretto is quite different:

> The point is to learn how to suffer, with love. So many people suffer with hatred in their hearts . . . But he who suffers with love has the power to save the world . . . The Christian does not reason like the Marxist, that one day there will be no more diseases, no more earthquakes, no more pain. The Christian understands the mystery of pain. He knows that there will always be a pit for people to fall into. We have to fill in as many pits as possible, yet never forget that there will always be a pit specially for me, and in it I must come to understand the mystery of the cross, which will lead to resurrection . . .

Carlo Carretto's whole life has been a 'waiting on God'. Like it or not, he says, life is a road, and along that road we have to learn how to wait. 'We must experience our own poverty, accept our own dark night, the fog that unexpectedly rises and blots out our sin.' The absolute basic essential is faith, the only way to hope and love. For himself he has only one desire: 'to die witnessing to Christ'.

MARY CRAIG
Woolton Hill
Newbury
Berkshire

God's call

God's call is mysterious; it comes in the darkness of faith. It is so fine, so subtle, that it is only with the deepest silence within us that we can hear it.

And yet nothing is so decisive and overpowering for a man on this earth, nothing surer or stronger.

This call is uninterrupted: God is always calling us.

But there are distinctive moments in this call of his, moments which leave a permanent mark on us – moments which we never forget.

Prayer is the most important thing. It is the hardest part of my daily life. Through my vocation to prayer I have learned what is meant by 'carrying other people'.

So after many years I can say that I have remained true to my vocation, and at the same time I am convinced that one never wastes one's time by praying: there is no more helpful way of helping those people we love.

Transformation into God

God does not hurry over things: time is his, not mine.

And I, little creature, man, have been called to be transformed into God by sharing his life. And what transforms me is the love which he pours into my heart.

Love transforms me slowly into God. But sin is still there, resisting his transformation, knowing how to, and actually saying 'no' to love.

Living in our selfishness means stopping at human limits and stopping our transformation into divine love. And until I am transformed, sharing the life of God, through love, I shall be 'of this earth', and not 'of that heaven'.

Baptism has raised me to the supernatural state but we must grow in this state, and the purpose of life is that growth. And love, or rather, God's love is what transforms us.

In the presence of God

To place oneself before what seems to be bread and to say 'Christ is there, living and true', is pure faith. Nothing is more nourishing than pure faith and prayer in faith is real prayer.

'There is no pleasure in adoring the Eucharist', one novice used to say to me. But it is precisely the renunciation of all desire to satisfy the senses that makes prayer strong and real. One meets God beyond the senses, beyond the imagination, beyond nature.

This is crucial: as long as we pray only when and how we want to, our life of prayer is bound to be unreal. It will run in fits and starts. The slightest upset will be enough to destroy the whole edifice of our prayer-life . . .

Put yourself in front of Jesus as a poor man: not with any big ideas but with living faith. Remain motionless in an act of love before the Father. Do not try to reach God with your understanding. That is impossible. Reach him in love; that is possible.

The open door

If God exists, why evil? If God is love, why sorrow? If God is a Father, why death? If I have knocked, why has he not opened to me?

I used to think all this and more, when I was new to this school. But then, walking patiently, not allowing myself to become frightened off by the first difficulties, hounding his door with the determination of a man on a hunger strike, and, above all, believing his Gospel true and unrelenting, I began to see the way things are. I began to discover how God goes about what he is doing. I began to distinguish his stealthy footsteps.

I was no longer amazed that he treated me like the bride of the Song of Songs, that he escaped when I opened the door. It was for him to open it, not me, always in a hurry.

To wait on God

Only God is, only God knows, only God can do anything. This is the truth, and with the help of my faith I discover this more deeply every day.

God alone rules the cosmos, only God knows when I shall die, only God can convert China. Why try to take on responsibilities that are not ours, why be amazed if Islam has not yet discovered Christ, or if millions of our brethren adhere to Buddhism and are spiritually satisfied? The hour will come, and that in no way depends on me . . .

God comes first, not man. Mary herself could have died without seeing Christ, had God not decided that the moment for the incarnation had come.

The men of Galilee would have gone on fishing in the lake and attending the synagogue of Capernaum if he had not been there to say 'Come'. That is the truth we must learn through faith: to wait on God. And this attitude of mind is not easy. This waiting, this not making plans, this searching the heavens, this being silent, is one of the most important things we have to learn.

Self-abandonment

Giving my life to you, Lord, means accepting yours. Giving my soul to you, Lord, means accepting yours. And your soul is still in Gethsemane with our poverty. And your life is still nailed to the cross by our sin.

My life, if led remote from the vision, remote from the reality which you have lived and which you live in your Body, the Church, is useless, pagan life, a prey to delusion, weariness and death.

Yet, if I put my trust only in your resurrection, if I bypass your Gethsemane and cross, it would be dangerous, as this is mankind's Gethsemane and cross too.

If I think only of your incarnation, without accepting mine, I reduce your existence and mine to a blasphemous farce.

No, Jesus, if I give you my soul and my life, I am at the centre of your soul and your life.

Facing reality

I have no hesitation in saying that most of the suffering in our individual lives is due to the effort required of us to face reality, rather than to any of the genuine misfortunes that may befall us.

There are some people who go through life refusing to accept themselves. I have known women who would have been wonderful people, had it not been for the complex some minor physical defect produced in them. Some people cannot even cross the road without reflecting gloomily that they are too short, or a little overweight, or that their beauty is marred by a facial blemish or a nose that is out of proportion. It is sad to have to say so, but that is how it is.

The beatitude of poverty could liberate us from those forms of slavery too, and then, having been freed by Christ, we would be able to see the supreme beauty of the spirit shining in all its transparency, even in the face of a man who is physically deformed. That was how Pope Innocent III regained something of his optimism when he saw Francis – saw a man untrammelled by complexes, authentic through his total acceptance of himself, a man without a mask.

Darkness and light

Faith is neither a feeling nor a mental process; it is an act of self-surrender in the dark to a God who is indeed darkness as far as our human nature is concerned. And he is darkness not because of an absence of light, but rather because we are overwhelmed by the reverberations of a light to which we are yet unaccustomed, here in the restricted world of our own unfolding history.

The area in which reason and faith operate, and in which there is an interplay of light and shadow belonging to the two clearly distinct worlds, the visible and the invisible, is a terribly complex one. When the light which emanates from the cloud of unknowing reaches the earth on which we are journeying, it forms, as it were, a *mist* (St Paul) which surrounds everything and forces us to *feel our way* (Acts), putting us on our guard and inducing within us a continual state of anxious expectation.

An expectation which obliges us to fix our gaze on what lies ahead, and gives us a glimpse of the unexpected patch of sunlight which is to come. And it is on this uneven terrain that, sooner or later, God will be waiting for us, as he waited for Abraham, as he waited for Moses, as he waited for Job.

Love

It is love which gives everything its value. It makes sense of the difficulty of spending hours and hours on one's knees praying, while so many men need looking after in the world. And in the context of love we must view our inability to change the world, to wipe out evil and suffering.

It is love which must determine man's actions, love which must give unity to what is divided. Love is the synthesis of contemplation and action, the meeting-point between heaven and earth, between God and man.

I have known the satisfaction of unrestrained action, and the joy of contemplative life in the dazzling peace of the desert, and I repeat again St Augustine's words: 'Love and do as you will.'

Do not worry about what you ought to do. Worry about loving. Do not interrogate heaven repeatedly and uselessly, saying 'What course of action should I pursue?'.

Concentrate on loving instead.

A true perspective

For this is precisely our tragedy: we think we know, when in fact we know nothing; we think we can see, when in fact we are blind. What do *we* know of death, of eternity, of the purpose of things, of suffering, of what was before us, of what will be after us?

We imagine we have a plan, when in fact we have not; we believe we know what is good for us, when all the time we may be working to destroy it.

All too often, our one concern is to remain at home undisturbed, however dull and joyless it may have become.

We are afraid of adventure, of the new and the mysterious. If it were left in our hands, we would ask God to stay here on our level, when all the while our happiness depends on our moving upwards towards him. We would willingly ask him to spare us all suffering, though it is genuinely for our good that we should suffer a little.

What we lack is a true perspective, and this distorts the whole picture of our lives.

Love every creature

If only our hearts were always tender and our souls fresh when we look at creation. What a source of joy it would be on our pilgrimage. We can pass by and see, or we can pass by and not see; it depends on us.

Creation is like a message written on things, a story told in symbol, a source of conversation for our souls. But we have to learn how to read, listen and converse. We are in constant danger of our hearts turning into stone, either with old age or with the petrification of sin . . . We become the deaf mutes of the Gospel, and in that case only Jesus can cure us.

Loving nature, conversing with nature, is not something extraneous to our love for God; it is part of it, an essential ingredient.

God speaks to us, teaches us, gives us his first revelation, in the symbols of the created world. Later we shall receive the revelation in word and later still a direct personal revelation from God, but things still continue to reveal God, as God himself intended . . .

Not to look at nature, not to love it to the full, is to refuse to read a document God has specifically composed for us in his love.

The love of God

Freeing the gift of love! What a difficult undertaking for creatures like ourselves, willingly trapped as we are by sin, shut in by our selfishness. There is no limit to our self-deception. And the path once entered upon is so slippery that God has to treat us harshly to bring us back to our senses.

But there is no other way of opening our eyes. It has to be painful. How can we possibly entertain the idea that we are different from other men, when we shout, cry, feel afraid, lack determination and behave atrociously just like everyone else?

It is the purification of love, the refining fire which exposes our nakedness. And God himself, who is love, is not powerless. On the contrary, because he is love, he acts with greater determination.

If the soul cannot free itself by way of the cross, then it cannot be free. Pain purifies love. It makes it true, real, pure. And in addition it gets rid of what is not really love . . . It frees love from pleasure which falsifies it like a mask.

It makes it a gift freely given.

God loves you

Yes, God is there before you, watching you. His look is creative, capable of achieving the impossible. And just as he looked on the chaos at the beginning, hovered over the waters with the smile of his favour, and drew forth the cosmos, so, looking at you with the same favouring smile, he realizes the final purpose of creation: love.

Take courage, then: God loves you. I know you do not deserve it, so it is useless to go on saying so: the fact is, he loves you. I know you are tormented by doubts, but do not be afraid. He loves you, and his love is freely given. He does not love you for what you are worth; he loves you because, as God, he cannot help loving you: he is love.

Let yourself go; let him take hold of you.

He accepts you as a son.

The road of love

'He who loves must be ready to die. That is what I did, and I died for you. And my love for you is eternal, invincible.

'Do as I did, love as I loved, and you will know what the beatitude means. Remember that one act of mercy is worth more than one act of cunning, and that the diplomacy you put into your relationships is straw thrown to the wind.

'And do not forget that it is better to lose than to win, when to lose means to be humiliated before our brother.

'Do you want the secret of running swiftly on the road of love, of enjoying a great peace of heart? Here it is: seek the last place before him whom you love; lower yourself voluntarily, as I lowered myself, even though I was God. Concern yourselves with loving, not being loved; do not look for human glory, but for the service of men; do not go in for victimizing, which eats your heart out, but be happy to be a joyous hidden victim; do not believe in armed violence, not even the revolution; believe in the violence of love; do not worry about converting the world; worry about converting yourselves; the smaller and poorer you are, the happier you will be.

'When love crucifies you, remember I am near you.'

Where love reigns

The Kingdom of heaven signifies God with us. There could be no more exalting news for us. God is with me vitally – God is united to me. My life becomes divine life, my history sacred history . . .

It is a Kingdom that has been prepared for us 'since the foundation of the world' (Matthew 25:34) and which unfolds without signs to be observed (Luke 17:20). It is a Kingdom into which Christ has transferred us, delivering us from 'the dominion of darkness' (Colossians 1:2) and into which 'it is hard for those who have riches to enter' (Luke 18:24).

It is a Kingdom where 'he who is least is greater than John' (Luke 7:28) and where our names are written in heaven (Luke 10:20). It is a Kingdom which was like a grain of mustard seed at first and then 'it grew and became a tree, and the birds of the air made nests in its branches' (Luke 13:19), and where 'men will come from east and west and from north and south, and sit at table' (Luke 13:29).

All this we know from the Gospel. But we also know that the Kingdom is more than a place or a legislative entity; it is a person – Jesus.

'Yes' to God

The Kingdom of God is really an act of love, and love is only possible in reciprocal acceptance – in a 'yes' pronounced by both. The project becomes a project in common. Once God became man, man became divine. Once God prepares the banquet, man is the indispensable guest.

God's action is vain unless the human being responds. John sees them in such a union, such an inseparable entity, that he uses the example of the grapevine: 'I am the vine, you are the branches' (John 15:5).

The visible fruit is on the branch. The branch is the human being. The invisible sap is the invisible life-giving presence of God within the human being. ' . . . cut off from me you can do nothing', says Jesus (John 15:5), proclaiming the presence of the divine within the human. But he also says to mankind, 'You are the light of the world' (Matthew 5:14), to affirm the factual importance of mankind in making the Kingdom visible.

The triumph of love

In our lives we receive insults and abuse from others but we rather tend to enjoy being a victim. We like to think that the pain is unbearable, because it seems to affect the roots of our being, our relationship with God and with our neighbour.

How can I love, really love my brother who sees me working day after day and repays me with indifference, and even with derision? How can I feel at ease . . . where my brethren have not taken my personality seriously and have not understood my abilities? Why should I still work with enthusiasm when someone has been promoted who does not really deserve it?

In fact, I no longer love: I am unable to. But this inability to love is quite crucial because it leaves me with an enormous feeling of indifference. . . Love is the aim of my life, the reason for my existence, the only thing that really satisfies me . . .

The Lord loves a happy giver . . . God will be the happy giver in his Christ. His gift of himself is unconditional. He will pardon all sins for ever. He will give life again to the tired bones of the sinner, he will transform a prostitute into a Mary Magdalene and an ordinary pleasure-seeker into a St Francis. Life will triumph over death and spring will find strength and beauty in the dung of the earth itself. I have overcome the world, Christ will shout in his sacrifice, and joy will flow again in our anguished hearts.

The fire of the Holy Spirit

Charity is God's way of loving; it is God's love itself. It is a person who is called Holy Spirit. It is the love which unites the Father with the Son. It is the love which penetrated us at Pentecost.

We are baptized no longer in water, but in the fire of the Holy Spirit – that is, in love. He who possesses the Holy Spirit and listens to him, understands everything; he who does not possess him and does not listen, understands nothing.

Light and darkness in our spirits are formed by this Spirit. When he came down upon the chaos this Spirit created the universe. When he covered Mary of Nazareth with his shadow, the flesh of the woman became the flesh of the Son of God.

The secret of poverty

The poor man is really poor, but the poor of Yahweh has God at his disposal.

The realization is enough to make one's head spin. God at the disposal of my faith! What an awesome thought!

Jesus has left us an echo of that sense of vertigo. We are told in the Gospel of his being tempted by the possibility of changing stones into bread, or of casting himself from the pinnacle of the temple without doing himself any harm. He says himself that he recovered his equilibrium by crying out in the midst of temptation: 'You must not put the Lord your God to the test' (Matthew 4:7). Yes, it is a terrible thing to feel that God is at the disposal of our poverty.

All things are possible for him who believes. That is the secret of the poor of Yahweh. I am nothing, but God is my all. *I have nothing, but God is the fullness of being and I will lose myself in him.* I believe this is the most radical experience man can have here on earth, the most dramatic struggle man can have with God, the face-to-face encounter of Israel with Yahweh in the night of the Passover under the moon of bare faith.

The lowest place

We are not happy because we are unforgiving, and we are unforgiving because we feel superior to others. Mercy is the fruit of the highest degree of love, because love creates equals, and a greater love makes us inferior.

First let us establish three premises: those who do not love feel superior to everyone else; those who love feel equal to everyone else; those who love much gladly take the lower place.

Each one of us can identify his position somewhere along this spectrum, which comprises the three degrees of the spiritual life here on earth: death for those who do not love; life for those who love; holiness for those who love much.

The beatitude of the merciful relates, like all the beatitudes, to the realm of holiness and we have to admit that Jesus set his sights high when he had the courage and confidence to place this lofty ideal before us. It is the beatitude that he himself lived to the full, stooping, out of love, to the lowest place, even to the extent of being rejected as a common criminal, fit only to be hung on a gibbet.

Poverty and love

Death was for Jesus the supreme moment of his supreme poverty. God had chosen the path of poverty to save man, and no moment of his journey was so steeped in poverty as the moment of his death. A dead God was absolute poverty: it was impossible to go further than that.

By reaching the depths of this dark abyss, Christ had reached all the people whom the Father had chosen to be his sons but who had forfeited this sonship through disobedience. By entering into the chaos produced by the perversity of a confused and deluded mankind, Jesus had identified himself with what was lost through showing that there was salvation even for sin.

By taking hardness-of-heart into its embrace, the power of love had been able to melt it. The prodigal son's flight had become a positive act because it brought to light the depths of the father's mercy. Love had won, man was saved. Freedom had inherited the earth.

Small before God

We must make ourselves small before God, as small as possible, as small as David who believed absolutely that he could not be beaten by Goliath, as small as Joseph who never disputed the angel's orders, as small as Mary who accepted with unswerving simplicity the improbable betrothal of herself and the Spirit of God, the incredible conception within her of Jesus the Christ. 'Blessed is she who believed' (Luke 1:45): therein lies Mary's greatness – and ours too, if we learn to believe and hope.

There is no other test of greatness. Looking at a piece of bread on the altar and saying 'That is Christ', is pure faith. Noting and listing all the sins of the people of God and its leaders and still letting oneself be guided by the mystery of the Church and its infallibility is a formidable thing; knowing that our bodies rot in the grave and yet believing in the resurrection of the body is a tremendous last test of life.

The successful candidate is the one who has made himself small and does not treat God's mysteries as though they were coins in his pocket.

Things great and small

One of the hardest battles in the spiritual life, perhaps I should say the hardest, is the struggle to see God in our trivial human happenings. How often we have to renew our act of faith! At first we are tempted to see only ourselves, to believe only in ourselves, to value only ourselves. Then gradually we perceive that the thread of life has a rationale, a mysterious unity, and we are led to think that we meet God in its basic stages.

Then again, as our religious experience grows, we begin to realize that we meet God not only in the big events of our lives but in all the events, however small and apparently insignificant.

God is never absent from our lives, he cannot be, because 'in him we live, and move, and exist' (Acts 17:28). But it requires so much effort to turn this truth into a habit!

We need repeated acts of faith before we learn to sail with confidence on the 'immense and endless sea' which is God (St Gregory Nazianzen), knowing that if we founder we do so in him, the divine, eternal, ever-present God. How fortunate we are if we can learn to navigate our frail craft on this sea and remain serene even when the storm is raging!

Entering the desert

I have come into the desert to pray, to learn to pray. It has been the Sahara's great gift to me and I should like to share it with all my friends. It is immeasurable and contains every other gift within itself. It is the *sine qua non* of life, the treasure buried in the field, the pearl of great price discovered in the market.

Prayer is the sum of our relationship with God. We are what we pray.

The degree of our faith is the degree of our prayer. The strength of our hope is the strength of our prayer. The warmth of our charity is the warmth of our prayer. No more nor less.

Our prayer has had a beginning because we have had a beginning. But it will have no end. It will accompany us into eternity and will be completed in our contemplation of God, when we join the harmony of heaven and are 'filled with the flood of God's delights'. The story of our earthly-heavenly life will be the story of our prayer. Thus above all it is a personal story.

Into the wilderness

In the Gospel the desert marks a period of preparation for Christ as he stands on the threshold of his active mission: 'Immediately afterwards the Spirit drove him out into the wilderness and he remained there for forty days and was tempted by Satan. He was with the wild beasts, and the angels looked after him' (Mark 1:12–13).

It provides some respite from the pressure of the crowd: 'Then he said to them, "You must come away to some lonely place all by yourselves and rest for a while" ' (Mark 6:31).

It is a milieu suited to prayer: 'After sending the crowds away he went up into the hills by himself to pray' (Matthew 14:23); or to prolonged meditation: 'Now it was about this time that he went out into the hills to pray; and he spent the whole night in prayer to God' (Luke 6:12); or to quench the thirst for absolute aloneness with the Father: ' "Stay here while I pray." And going on a little further he threw himself on the ground and prayed that, if it were possible, this hour might pass him by. "Abba [Father]" ' (Mark 14:32–35).

Creating a desert

If the prophets did so, and if Jesus did so, we too must go out into the desert from time to time.

It is not a question of transporting oneself there physically. For many of us that could be a luxury. Rather, it implies creating a desert space in one's own life. And to create a desert means to seek solitude, to withdraw from men and things, one of the undisputed principles of mental health.

To create a desert means learning to be self-sufficient, learning to remain undisturbed with one's own thoughts, one's own prayer, one's own destiny.

It means shutting oneself up in one's room, remaining alone in an empty church, setting up a small oratory for oneself in an attic or at the end of a passage in which to localize one's personal contact with God, to draw breath, to recover one's inner peace. It means occasionally devoting a whole day to prayer, it means going off into the loneliness of the mountains, or getting up alone in the night to pray.

When all is said and done, creating a desert means nothing more than obeying God. Because there is a commandment – arguably the most forgotten of all, especially by the 'committed', by militants, by priests, and even bishops – which requires us to interrupt our work, to put aside our daily tasks and seek the refreshing stillness of contemplation.

The desert in crowded places

To encourage you, let me tell you that at the time of my conversion I made the train the 'place' for my prayer. My work took me back and forth, and you know what a railway carriage is like when you go to and from the city every morning and evening – cram full of workers and students. Noise, laughter, smoke, bustle, crush.

I sat in a corner and heard nothing. I read the Gospel. I closed my eyes. I spoke and listened to God. What sweetness, what peace, what silence! The power of love overcame the distractions that sought to penetrate my fortress.

I really was at one with myself and nothing could have distracted me. I was at peace in the hands of love. Yes, it must have been love to create such unity within me. Indeed, the lovers who were in the train whispered to each other in perfect harmony, unaware of what was going on around them.

I whispered to my God whom I had rediscovered. 'Poustinia'. To create the desert in crowded places. To make a railway carriage a place of meditation, to make the streets of my city into the corridors of my ideal convent.

Sharing the life of God

God offers himself in three ways: his Spirit, his presence and his revelation of himself. And for these three offers he asks of man but one thing: 'If a man loves me.'

The man who offers God his love becomes 'paradise on earth', the Trinity is a reality within him: he is an instrument of the Spirit and of God's will.

These three ways of God offering himself to us are possible because of the death and resurrection of Christ, and are a reality because of him. It is through prayer that we absorb this reality, for prayer establishes us in the deepest possible relationship with God. By our prayer we share the life of God.

The Trinity becomes a reality within us as the guest of the soul. Earth becomes heaven. Why go on searching for God beyond the stars when he is so close to us, within us? Heaven, this hidden place, is not some lofty, vaulting construction, studded with stars. It is a land of intimate closeness, so near that we can speak to God, stay with him, worship him anywhere.

His Holy Spirit is in us.

Man's potentiality

Jesus told the parable of the prodigal son with each of us in mind, knowing that each of us would live our individual version of the story. And he loves us as we are, at whatever stage of our journey. He loves the potentiality in us. The potentiality for conversion, return, love, light. He loves the Magdalene when she is still a sinner, because he already sees her gradual progress towards the light as something marvellous, as something worth serious attention here on earth.

He loves Zacchaeus the sinner, robber, exploiter, and finds it good that such a man can be capable of reversing his conduct and becoming a friend of the poor. Yes, God loves what in man is not yet. What has still to come to birth. What we love in a man is what already is: virtue, beauty, courage, and hence our love is self-interested and fragile.

God, loving what is not yet and putting his faith in man, continually begets him, since love is what begets. By giving man confidence, he helps him to be born, since love is what helps us to emerge from our darkness and draws us into the light. And this is such a fine thing to do that God invites us to do the same.

The ability to hope

The ability to hope is the greatest gift that God could make to man. When man is endowed with hope, he overcomes the obstacles in which he is ensnared. When man hopes, he dies already seeing his body in the resurrection light.

When man hopes, he overcomes fear, understands the purpose of the ordeal, puts his trust in God, believes in things which are impossible, feels God's presence in his darkness, begins to pray. Abraham's hope is one of the wonders of mankind, and the hope of the martyrs is the radiance of the Church.

Hope is born when man experiences the abyss of his helplessness, as Israel did in Babylon, as Jeremiah when lowered into the prison cistern, as Jesus on the cross. And now I approach Jesus Forsaken with greater understanding. In him, I see all the world's sufferings concentrated, the redemptive fire of mankind in evolution, the key to love's great secret.

Hidden God

Your servant Isaiah loved to describe you as a '*hidden God*' (Isaiah 45:15). You hide in the creation. You hide in history. You hide in the incarnation. You hide in the Eucharist. You hide within us. You hide all the time.

And you want us to discover you . . . like this . . . on our own . . . in our own time . . . when we need you. Generally, need is what impels us to seek you. The need for the absolute, for eternity, light, freedom, love. Above all, we seek you in our difficulties, when we no longer know which way to turn, when we are disillusioned by our pleasures. But even then you hide what you are doing and give us the impression that we ourselves are conducting the search.

I believe that your motive is always the same: you do not want to force us. You do not want a marriage of convenience, you do not want to damage our freedom. And when we get up and come to you, taking the road prepared by you from the outset, we feel perfectly free.

Father and son

'The Father is in me and I am in him.' As a person. Being a person means seeing, knowing, loving, wishing; it means communicating. And what doubts can our faith entertain when the whole 'Word' tends to demonstrate it? Is not this the very mystery hidden throughout the centuries of the Old Dispensation, handed down to us by the prophets and confirmed for us by Christ?

If not so, why did Yahweh say to David, '*I shall be his Father and he will be my son*' (2 Samuel 7:14)? and to Solomon, '*I give you a wise and shrewd heart. Furthermore, I shall give you what you have not asked me for: riches and honour*' (1 Kings 3:12–13)? And faced with sick Hezekiah's plea, does not God reply, '*I have heard your prayer and tears; I shall cure you and in three days' time you will go up to the Temple of Yahweh*' (2 Kings 20:5)?

And when Isaiah was trying to express his prophetic hope, did not he say, '*Yahweh called me before I was born, before my birth he had pronounced my name. He made my mouth a sharp sword and hid me in the shadow of his hand. He made me into a sharpened arrow and concealed me in his quiver, saying to me, "You are my servant, Israel, through whom I shall manifest my glory"*' (Isaiah 49:1–3)? If from the Bible and particularly from the Gospel you exclude this mode of being, this personal relationship between God and man, you completely abandon Tradition, the plain sense of the Word. And experience of God too!

True spiritual childhood

Yes, love has reduced us to nothing. It has taken from us all presumption of knowing or being. It has reduced us to true spiritual childhood.

I have held my soul
In peace and silence
As a child
In its mother's arms.

This is the highest state of prayer; to be children in God's arms, silent, loving, rejoicing.

And if through desire of yours to say something, or do something, you feel that you must open your mouth, then do this: choose one word or a little phrase which well expresses your love for him. And then go on repeating it in peace, without trying to form thoughts, motionless in love before God, who is love.

And with this word or this phrase transformed into an arrow of steel, a symbol of your love, beat again and again against God's thick cloud of unknowing.

The contemplation of God

The nature of contemplation is passive. It comes from beyond. When I contemplate I do not look inside myself, I look ahead of me.

What do my ideas matter? I know them and they die one after the other. What engages me in contemplation is an idea that cannot die, and this comes from God. That is why I believe in contemplation.

One ounce of transcendence is dearer to me than any amount of reasoning. If reasoning is there at all, it comes beforehand. All my life I have been reasoning. Now I am trying to do without reasoning for a time while I lay myself before God and let him act upon me . . .

Contemplation is passive; it is God's coming into us, into our consciousness. God lets us know him as he is, not as he may appear to be from outside. In contemplation, I attain the fullness of my earthly life and I feed on eternal life, because eternal life is what I am destined for. All the rest can take care of itself, because it counts for little compared with eternal life.

Contemplation in the streets

Contemplation in the streets. This is tomorrow's task not only for the Little Brothers but for all the poor.

Let us begin to analyse this element of 'desert' which must be present, especially today in carrying out such a demanding programme. When one speaks of the soul's desert and says that the desert must be present in your life, you must not think only of the Sahara or the desert of Judea or of the High Valley of the Nile.

Certainly it is not everyone who can have the advantage of being able to carry out in practice this detachment from daily life. The Lord conducted me into the real desert because I was so thick-skinned. For *me* it was necessary. But all that sand was not enough to erase the dirt from my soul; even the fire was not enough to remove the rust from Ezekiel's pot.

One hour a day, one day a month, eight days a year, for longer if necessary, you must leave everybody and everything and retire, alone with God. If you do not look for this solitude, if you do not love it, you will not achieve real contemplative prayer.

But the desert is not the final stopping-place. It is a stage on the journey. Because our vocation is contemplation in the streets. You must go back among men, mix with them, live your intimacy with God in the noise of their cities. It will be difficult, but you must do it. And for this the grace of God will not fail you.

The attitude of prayer

Prayer is faith in action, the well-spring of hope, the conversation of love. There is no substitute when we truly want to possess eternal life, when we really become conscious of God.

Anyone who does not pray cannot know God's intimate life (which in theology is called charity). He can only know him from the outside, as a symbol, as an idea, as a philosophy, as a science, as a number, as space, as eternity.

It is not enough to study theology or advanced exegesis to know God.

God's intimate life is unknowable to man.

He is 'veiled' to man.

He only makes himself knowable, he only unveils himself, when we come before him in an attitude of love, not in an attitude of curiosity.

Prayer, true prayer, is precisely the attitude in which man must present himself before God in order to enter his intimate life, which is the life of the Trinity.

Prayer as listening

At this point let us call to mind one very important thing: prayer is not so much a matter of talking as listening; contemplation is not watching but being watched.

On the day when we realize this, we will have entered finally into possession of the truth, and prayer will have become a living reality. To be watched by God: that is how I would define contemplation, which is passive rather than active, more a matter of silence than of words, of waiting rather than of action.

What am I before God? What can I do to be worthy of his revelation? If he shuts, no one opens, and if he opens, no one shuts. He is the active principle of love, he is before all, he is the one who makes within me his own prayer, which then becomes my prayer.

I do not know what has happened or is happening within you, but I do know what has happened and is happening within myself, and I can tell you this: that it was he who sought me in the first place, and it is he who continues to seek me.

Prayer and one's neighbour

If you pray, if you pray seriously, if you pray in truth, it will be God himself who will send you out, with greater strength, with greater love, towards your brothers, so that you may love them more gratuitously and serve them more delicately. Well then, you will say, why, why in the past have too many Christians scandalized me with their indifference, with the hardness of their bigoted hearts, with the hermetic sealing of themselves against every problem of justice and liberation of the people?

Yet they were praying, they were contemplating! No, if they were praying, their prayer was just a bit of rhetoric. If they were contemplating, they were contemplating . . . nothing. They were deceiving you, and they were deceiving the Church.

It is impossible to pray to a personal God – that is, love a personal God – and remain indifferent to your suffering brethren. It is impossible. Anyone who prays without suffering for his suffering brothers is praying to a pole, a shadow, not to the living God. Because if you pray to the living God, you who are living, he, the Living One, sends you to your living brothers.

Possession

Possessiveness is one of the most insidious temptations. By being possessive about things you take away their transparency, their freedom, their identity. By being possessive about creation you become its slave.

Each thing has its own vocation, and freedom is the voice of vocation. I had my son Jesus, but my son Jesus was perfectly free and our love developed with reciprocal freedom. How difficult it is to live the life of love without falling into possessiveness – which is slavery. And we are called to freedom. For us Nazareth was the school of freedom and Jesus was freedom.

It was this that taught us and kept us going: freedom from money, freedom from idols, freedom from public opinion, freedom from fear, freedom from everything. We had to possess as if we did not possess, mourn as though we were not mourning, rejoice as if we were not rejoicing (cf. 1 Corinthians 7:30). In our little home we felt that 'all are yours; and you are Christ's; and Christ is God's' (1 Corinthians 3:23).

The apostolate

But the first thing I must understand and believe is *that my work is of enormous value, that the duties incumbent on me as a human being are holy because they are willed by God and I fulfil them in obedience to his Law.* And if God allows me a little free time after all the work and chores, I can devote a few minutes to contemplation, enabling my life to achieve its proper balance.

People say: 'I've got too much on in my apostolate, I can't pray.' Now the contradiction here is so obvious that only Manzoni's word is adequate: our poor hearts are nothing but a 'jumble'.

How can there be any opposition between two ways of expressing love for the same Person? If prayer is love for God, how can it be excluded from another form of love for God, the apostolate?

Love is for living

My life is worth living if I can learn to transform everything that happens to me into love, in imitation of Jesus: because *love is for living.*

When I have to live with people who do not see things the way I see them, who say they are enemies of my faith, I shall love them, and in loving them I shall sow the seeds of future dialogue in my heart and theirs: because *love is for living.*

When I see time's destructive traces in my body and the approach of old age, I shall try to love even more in order to transform the coldest season of life into a total gift of myself in preparation for the imminent holocaust: because *love is for living.*

When I see the evening of my life, or, on the tarmac in a car accident, in the agony of a fatal illness, in the ward of a geriatric hospital, feel the end coming, I shall reach out again for love, striving to accept in joy whatever fate God has had in store for me: because *love is for living.*

Love without keeping accounts

Do you want to know the secret of true happiness? Of deep and genuine peace? Do you want to solve at a blow all your difficulties in relations with your neighbour, bring all polemic to an end, avoid all dissension?

Well, decide here and now to love things and men as Jesus loved them, that is, to the point of self-sacrifice. Do not bother with the book-keeping of love; love without keeping accounts.

If you know someone who is decent and likeable, love him, but if someone else is very *un*likeable, love him just the same. If someone greets you and smiles, greet him and smile back, but if someone else treads on your feet, smile just the same. If someone does you a good turn, thank the Lord for it, but if someone else slanders you, persecutes you, curses you, strikes you, thank him and carry on.

Do not say: 'I'm right, he's wrong.' Say: 'I must love him as myself.' This is the kind of love Jesus taught: a love which transforms, vivifies, enriches, brings peace.

Free from fear

It may well be that the Church will have hard times, as Israel had at the time of the Babylonian Captivity – many harsh, straight-speaking prophecies circulate in the undergrowth of our parishes. For myself, this does not worry me very much, since Christ himself has set me free from fear; hence I am no longer in Israel's position, to be terrorized by the Assyrian sword.

I feel myself reassured and comforted by the coming of Jesus into my life and, as I search the works of Hosea, I prefer to linger over these sayings of his: 'Ephraim, how could I part with you? Israel, how could I give you up? My whole being shudders at the thought – for I am God, and not man' (Hosea 11:8–9).

Behold, I am your God, says the Lord. And to be God, my God, means that he is my Father, that he is the root of my existence, that he is the Lord of heaven and earth, that he is the Absolute, that he is the Saviour, that he is my End and my All.

If God is my God, I need fear nothing. I put my trust in him. I let myself go. He is the God of the impossible.

Created things

When I was younger and more impatient I used to get bored, when the junior scouts opened their tents and gazed curiously and affectionately at the woods and at the tiny animals under the yellowing leaves. It seemed a waste of time. I would have preferred to have had them taught catechism in some church.

I was immature and did not understand that the best catechism is to fix our eyes on created things, because through things God begins to speak to us. It may be, through teaching catechism to bored students sitting on benches, teaching abbreviated formulas and intellectual summaries, that we have destroyed everything, leaving them sad and absent before the mystery of God.

Today, so many years later, how I would like to replace a catechism lesson with a walk in the fields, offering to a boy who lives buried in the inhuman cemetery of the city, the wonderful discovery of a sparrow's nest.

For is not wonder the first unconscious meeting with mystery? Does not wonder give birth to the first prayer? Does not the power to contemplate involve first the power to be awed?

The signs of creation

God embraces you through the wind that blows back your hair and he kisses you with the first rays of the morning sun. The tools of your daily work can be the touch of God's hands, and his greeting the whistle of the train that passes over the viaduct by your house. If you do not want the signs of creation all around you to distract you, then fill them with the presence of God.

They will speak to you of him. If you want the streets that you pace to become the corridors of your favourite convent, then see them in the light of his presence. Your work will no longer be a burden, separating you from prayer, if you carry it out as an act of obedience to his Word resounding in your ears: 'In the sweat of your face you shall eat bread' (Genesis 3:19). And men, with their infinite contradictions, will cease to be instruments of distraction if you try to see them as Jesus saw them and feel for them as he felt for them: 'I have compassion on the crowd' (Mark 8:2).

God's presence which comes to you by means of signs will transform the environment where you live into a temple where you will be able to 'worship God in spirit and in truth' (John 4:24). How can there be a more living desert than yours if you see it as inhabited by the Living God?

Nature's balance

Man is free to indulge in riotous living and to live by overthrowing the order of things, but on his way he will surely meet the suffering that will prostrate him. He is free to separate himself from God who is order, nature and life, but God then surrounds him with a hedge and fills his path with thorns so that he sees that it is better to stop and perhaps even turn round and go back again.

Nature is one of God's great signs and man will never manage to elude it. Nor will he succeed in ridding himself of the fear, indeed the terror, that death lays upon him. In the last analysis, what matters is to stop in time.

I am reminded of the story of Pinocchio. He is made of wood so is insensitive to pain. But when he let his leg loll in the fireplace near the fire, his insensitivity to pain became a great danger and threatened his life. It seems absurd to say it, but: what would happen if there were no pain to sensitize us in time, to warn us?

The truth of God and man

There are times when God makes us feel the extreme limits of our powerlessness; then and only then do we understand our nothingness right down to our depths. For so many years, for too many years, I have fought against my powerlessness, my weakness. Often I have refused to admit it to myself, preferring to appear in public with a nice mask of self-assurance.

Now I do not fight any more. I try to accept myself. I try to face up to myself without illusions, dreams or fantasies. It is a step forward, I believe. And if I had made the step while I was still learning the catechism, I should have gained forty years. I seem to have reached a means of encountering him in a way I have never known before; a togetherness I have never experienced before, an awareness of his love I had never felt previously. Yes, it is my misery which attracts his power, my wounds which shout after him, my nothingness which makes him throw himself open to me.

And this meeting between God's totality and man's nothingness is the greatest wonder of creation. It is the most beautiful betrothal because its bond is a love which gives itself freely and a love which accepts. Really it is the truth of God and man. The acceptance of this truth comes from humility, and that is why without humility there is no truth, and without truth no humility.

God of the impossible

God can do everything and I can do nothing. But if I offer this nothing in prayer to God, everything becomes possible to me.

Within myself I feel the ability to perform an act of perfect love following Jesus on Calvary, dying with him on the cross.

Thousands and thousands of years may pass and my position will not change.

But . . . what is impossible for me, the rich man in the Gospel, is possible for God! It is he who will give me the grace to transform myself; he will make me able to carry out the impossible and remove the obstacle which separates me from the Kingdom.

And so it is a question of waiting, of humble and trustful prayer, of patience and hope.

But the God of the impossible will not ignore my cry.

God's covenant with mankind

God wanted a covenant with mankind: this covenant is both the content and the goal of the whole plan of salvation. But a covenant must be made between the living and not the dead, and between persons and not concepts or symbols.

If the truth is that God, in his mercy, has desired an alliance with me, he must enter upon my road where I can meet him.

Personal prayer is the meeting-place between the Eternal One and me: the Blessed Sacrament is the visible sign of my covenant with him.

This is why I believe in personal prayer and why every day I wait to meet him in the Eucharist. To pray means to wait for the God who comes. Every prayer-filled day sees a meeting with the God who comes; every night which we faithfully put at his disposal is full of his presence.

And his coming and his presence are not only the result of our waiting or a prize for our efforts: they are his decision, based on his love freely poured out. God is thrust onward by his love, not attracted by our qualities. He comes even in moments when we have done everything wrong, when we have done nothing . . . when we have sinned.

Eyes to see

We say we want faith, but we do not want to open our purses to the poor. We claim we are looking for Christ, but we make no effort to change our lives, even though we can see how mistaken they are.

I feel I must give the lie to the man who says 'I'm looking for God, but I can't find him'. Let him try to do everything in the truth, free from the demon of pride and the suffocating density of egoism. Let every trace of racism be rooted out, let every man be welcomed as a brother, and . . . you will see, you will see!

Live love. Act truth. Honour life. And it will be God within you that you live, act, and honour. God will not come to you because you have been 'good'. He was already there. He has always been coming and always is coming. But now you can see him because you have purified your eyes, softened your heart, and stooped down.

Remember he was already there. He was already there. He was already there. The only difficulty was that you were unable to see him.

The life of faith

The life of faith is the most extraordinary thing that exists on earth; it casts into shadow the gifts we received formerly, just as the gift of becoming man cast into shadow the gift of being born to light.

With faith I become a participant in God's life, entering a new orbit, the orbit of God. With faith I pass through the heavens, travel in the invisible, conquer the strength of my human nature, overcome my weakness, become a son of God.

This is so extraordinary that there is no limit to its grandeur or the possibilities of its development. Faith enables me to conquer fear, to overcome death. It is invincible. St John says: 'The power that has conquered the world is this faith of ours' (1 John 5:4).

Indeed, what is left to fear if God is my Father? What possibility can worry me, if I conclude with the most extraordinary possibility that can be imagined: eternal life? The fullness of the Kingdom? The resurrection of the dead? The *agape* of all redeemed men with God himself at the table?

The God of faith

The God of faith is not a God who is silent, a God who is inactive, a God who is not present to us.

To you who are a person, he is a person; to you who have life, he is life; to you who have love, he is love. He is the 'Other' who is searching for you.

He has always been searching for you.

And you are looking for the 'Other', even when – and it often happens – you feel you are doing something quite different.

In the end everything we do on this earth is pushed on solely by this search for the 'Other'. We search for him first in things. Then in creatures, with even more intimate relationships. Finally, in the maturity of faith, the 'Other' shows himself to us as a transcendent and autonomous presence, detached from things and creatures beyond creation: the Absolute.

I can never insist enough that this beginning of the life of faith is governed by God himself. It is his gift, and we cannot anticipate it by a single instant, however many mountains of virtue we may heap up.

It is a freely given gift.

Faith, a relationship with God

. . . Faith is a new dimension at work in us, one which does not start from reason, surpasses it infinitely because it can reach God: in faith, the soul is invited to establish a living relationship with God, to see him, listen to him and speak with him.

Abraham is the ancestral head of all men of faith, of all those whose lives enjoy this new dimension, who accept the risks and the consequences. He is the founder of the family of believers, he stands at the head of the 'people of God', those mysterious folk who puncture reality and carry on beyond things, who hear the voices coming from the other side, who travel beyond time into eternity, looking for the Absolute, the Infinite, who consider themselves to be exiles on earth, perpetual nomads, who are not satisfied with what they can see but look for the invisible God, who learn to find him everywhere and who obey him as a King, as a Tremendous Lover.

In short, Abraham is the model of those who respond to God's call.

God and man

The taking of Adam's rib for the creation of Eve foretells the unbreakable union between man and wife. In the same way, the imagery of Jacob's struggle encodes the entire mystery of prayer as a combat of love between man and God, the creature wrestling with his Creator.

Man wants to pass but God does not let him pass, although he wants him to pass.

Man wrestles with God and God is happy to see man's shoulder pressing on his own heart. Man asks God to say 'Yes' and God refrains from saying it, just to hear the infinite repetition of the request, louder every time.

The struggle on the bridge of passage, and the dialectic of love between God and man, between Yahweh and Israel, is the ever-maturing awareness of man's 'Yes' and God's eternal 'Yes'.

God resists man, because man's desire is still superficial, immature, childish. God lets man weep because man still needs to weep. He lets man wait because man still needs to wait. Union is not yet mature, desire still lacks clarity.

A great struggle is still necessary and the night is night just for this. The daybreak will come and everything will change.

The presence of God

I am a dwelling-place. I am not alone.

In the secret depths of my poor human substance is the presence of God. Not a God who is a solitary, but a God who is Trinity, a God who is love.

A God who is Father, a God who is Son, a God who is Holy Spirit. But a God made one by love.

And a God whose love enables me to become one with him: 'that you may be one as you, Father, are in me, and I in you, I pray that they may be one in us, that the world may believe that you sent me' (John 17:21).

I believe that no moment exists for man which is more important, more beautiful, more dramatic, more decisive, more radical than the moment when he becomes aware of – or, rather, 'lives' – this reality.

When God reveals himself in his nature as one and in his actions as three, Pentecost penetrates the depths of men's hearts.

Divisions in the hearts of men

A few days ago I revisited the Berlin Wall – that absurdity that lasts and lasts while life goes on around it as if nothing were the matter. I realized as never before that that wall is but one outward sign of an infinite number of other walls, the walls that divide up people and things. The real wall is within us, and it divides rich from poor, nation from nation, children from parents, human beings from one another, human beings from God.

We are divided, split apart to the depths of our innards, as the Berlin Wall divides Germans from Germans, as Jerusalem is split between Jews and Arabs, as any man or woman may be all alone in the universe around.

Everything is quiet, for the moment – but all ready to explode.

Yes, I truly believe we could be on the eve of the apocalypse – unless . . .

The demands of justice

The struggle against injustice and outrage, especially those committed against the poor and defenceless, is a basic Christian duty, and Christians are not permitted to be silent, to withdraw, to refuse to get involved. If they understood, really understood, they would volunteer to die for justice.

That is what Jesus did. But nowhere is it written that, to make your adversary yield, it is necessary or indispensable to employ the sword, the machine-gun, or the tank. The highest claim of the Gospel is that I can cause my enemy to yield with my unarmed love, with my bare hand, as Gandhi did, as Martin Luther King did, as all who believe in nonviolence do, as Bishop Romero did in your day.

What a sublime example this unarmed man gave! What wonderful words he spoke against the mighty, still massacring his people! Give a handful of men and women like that – give the Church a band of heroes with strength like that – and then you will realize that when Jesus proposed nonviolence he was not doing so to lose battles. He was doing so to win them, and win them in the only way worthy of a human being: without shedding the blood of others, but by shedding one's own.

I sought and I found

You! I! What should I be without you? But what would you be without me? What would Jesus be without the Father? And really . . . can you imagine the Father without Jesus? The mystical Reality is the Relationship, and the Relationship is called the Holy Spirit. 'My Father goes on working, and so do I' (John 5:17).

There are not two mysteries: God, and man. There is only one, and both are one, and always found together. I cannot disconnect myself from my God. He is the being of my being, the root of my root, and all things converge on the unity of Being. And hence, a woman's womb with a child in it is the best simile we have for the relationship between God and man, the sign best symbolizing that reality.

No longer seek God far away from you. Seek him within yourself and abide in his presence. Let yourself go. Let God act. But your letting-go must be perpetual activity, like a road unmoving yet leading on to somewhere, like a 'yes' pronounced in concert, deliberately, for ever. God is what you seek as perfection, as being, as oneness, as love.

I sought – yes, I sought, for he was seeking me. That is my answer. I found him because he was already there, waiting for me.

The ultimate self-abandonment

Come then, death! Come, I am waiting. You do not frighten me any more. I no longer see you as my foe. I see you as a sister. I look you in the face. I understand you now.

And as you come towards me, I tell you, thinking of him who holds you firmly in his mighty hand, '*Do with me what you will*'.

Accustom me to this extreme abandonment. Accustom me to this never-ending test, to this never-adult kiss, to this never-given change, to this never-finished conversation.

Accustom me little by little, by distributing my death through all the days of my life. Put it in my house as '*something lacking*', so that I do not accept the limitations of the visible. Put it as insecurity into my security, so that I may only be secure in him who is the Absolute. Put it as a reminder in the midst of my joys, so that I may grow used to being alone, as in that second when I shall be alone with you.

The meaning of death

To accept death as an act of love is not easy. And I believe that this was the climax of Christ's achievement in his travail towards love. And it is for us to imitate him, even in our weakness.

Real death is separation from God, and this is unbearable; real death is faithlessness, hopelessness, lovelessness. We all know what pain and sadness are, for we have all experienced them and are all immersed in them.

Real death is emptiness, darkness, desolation, despair, hatred, destruction. So . . . Christ agreed to enter into this death, into this separation, so as to identify himself with all who were in separation, and to save them.

When he had touched the depths of their despair, he announced hope with his resurrection. When he was immersed in their darkness, he made the brightness of truth burst forth with his resurrection. When engulfed in the abyss of their lovelessness, he showed them the infinite joy of love with his resurrection.

By rising from the dead, Christ made all things new. By rising from the dead, he opened new heavens. By rising from the dead, he opened new life.

Sources and index

In the index below, the figures in bold type refer to the pages of Readings in this book. For references to published works from which the Readings are taken, abbreviations are as follows:

BB: *Blessed Are You Who Believed*. Search Press 1982
DC: *The Desert in the City*. Collins/Fount 1979
GC: *The God Who Comes*. DLT 1974
IF: *I, Francis*. Collins/Fount 1982
IS: *I Sought and I Found*. DLT 1984
LD: *Letters from the Desert*. DLT 1972
LL: *Love is for Living*. DLT 1976
SB: *In Search of the Beyond*. DLT 1975
SL: *Summoned by Love*. DLT 1977
WL: *Why, O Lord?* DLT 1986

17 *LD* 123
18 *GC* 197–8
19 *SB* 35–6
20 *SB* 152
21 *BB* 51–2
22 *LL* 43–4
23 *LL* 109
24 *LD* 35
25 *SB* 18
26 *SB* 18–19
27 *DC* 20–21
28 *LD* 53
29 *SL* 98–9
30 *SL* 116–17
31 *SL* 48
32 *SL* 72
33 *LD* 61
34 *GC* 38
35 *LD* 72
36 *GC* 127–8
37 *SB* 76–7
38 *GC* 178–9
39 *BB* 38–9
40 *LL* 118
41 *LL* 135
42 *LL* 144
43 *SL* 17
44 *GC* 5
45 *DC* 42
46 *DC* 66
47 *LD* 133
48 *LD* 135
49 *GC* xvi
50 *GC* 17
51 *GC* 10
52 *GC* 27
53 *LL* 30–31
54 *GC* 50
55 *GC* 87
56 *IF* 13–14
57 *IF* 46–7
58 *IS* 82–3
59 *SL* 44–5
60 *BB* 52